A Christian Writer's Guide to...

The Book Proposal

DAVID E. FESSENDEN

What others are saying...

In order to get a book published, an author must write a salable book proposal, which can be as difficult as writing the actual book. Besides selling the book, a proposal acts as a road map to keep the author on track when writing the rest of the book. Dave Fessenden is a trusted voice in the world of Christian publishing.

In *A Christian Writer's Guide to the Book Proposal*, he tells you why you should write a book proposal, even if you already have a publishing contract or are self-publishing, and he teaches you how produce a professional-looking one.

Susan Titus Osborn, director of The Christian Communicator Manuscript Critique Service and author of more than thirty books.

If you've ever cringed at the thought of doing a book proposal, Dave Fessenden understands. Go from "I have to" to "I get to" as you read his practical, doable, steps and soak up his fresh insights. This book will help you, no matter what your genre is or where you are in the process.

Shirley Leonard, author, *With Each Passing Moment: Help and Hope for Caregivers*.

Stop! Before you even write one word, read this book! Author Dave Fessenden makes the case that the proposal should come first, and that writing it can actually be enjoyable. Dave's invaluable wisdom saves countless hours of Googling "How to write a killer book proposal." It gives writers the how-to and examples they need to catch the editor's eye and nail down the ever-elusive publishing deal.

Janelle Leonard, novelist, and blogger at The Writing Life: Behind the Scenes with an Author of YA Fantasy

A Christian Writer's Guide to the Book Proposal
Published by Sonfire Media, LLC
© 2015 by David E. Fessenden
All rights reserved.
Printed and bound in the United States of America

For information contact:

Sonfire Media, LLC
974 East Stuart Drive
Suite D, PMB 232
Galax, VA 24333

Cover & Interior book design by Larry W. Van Hoose

ISBN No. 978-0-9891064-5-0

Contents

Employ your time

in improving yourself by other men's writings,

so that you shall gain easily what others labored hard for.

Socrates

Why Do a Proposal, Anyway?

God has given you a great idea for a book. Maybe you've already gathered some notes, perhaps even written a few chapters, or completed a rough draft. Well, if you're like most authors, you're more or less stuck at this point. You have a major case of writer's block on your hands, and you wonder if you'll ever get past it.

Let me make a suggestion. Before you write one more word, do yourself a favor: prepare a book proposal.

Most authors seem to approach the proposal process with a feeling of dread. It's probably the part of writing a book that they enjoy the least, and they seem to save it for last. But I'm here to tell you that writing the proposal ought to be the most enjoyable and invigorating part of the process, and something every author ought to do first—even before writing a rough draft.

Of course, if you're trying to get your book published by a traditional publisher (as opposed to one of the various forms of self-publishing), or if you are looking for an agent to take you on as a client, you *need* a book proposal. It's not just a nice thing to have—it's a necessity. For those who have any doubts about that, it is hard to get past the fact that most nonfiction books are contracted from a book proposal, often before a manuscript is fully written. Most fiction publishers and agents, on the other hand, will not send a contract on an uncompleted novel, especially from a first-time novelist. But they still make their decision based on the information in the book proposal. The purpose of the proposal is to sell the book, and that's what it does.

"That's all well and good, but I don't have to bother with it," you may say. "I've already got a contract," or, "I'm planning to self-publish." I have news for you, my friend. It's *still* to your advantage to prepare a book proposal!

Six Secret Advantages to Preparing a Proposal

There are secret benefits to a proposal that give your book project a much higher chance of success. It's to your advantage to write a proposal, even if you have a contract already, even if you are self-publishing. Here's why:

1. A proposal forces you to think through your book: How do I describe it, categorize it, and sell it to the reader? In preparing the proposal, you may discover that there's not as much *content* to your book idea as you previously thought. It may drive you back to doing more research and/or brainstorming, and the book ends up with a far richer message than it might have had.

2. It forces you to ask a tough question: Who would want to read this book? In other words, who is your audience? What particular groups of people are looking for a book like yours to meet a need in their life? I hear this statement from first-time authors: "People need to read my book." That may be true, but what kind of need are you talking about, and how does your book meet that need? You have to identify people who *know* they have that need and are looking to meet that need. Unless you aim the book at *that group of people*, it cannot be successful.

3. It forces you to ask another tough question: Has this idea been done before? What makes it distinctive? Let's be honest: maybe you are unconsciously putting together a cheap imitation of a book you read years ago. The proposal helps you sidestep that pitfall because it hones in on your book's unique features.

4. It forces you to start thinking about marketing and promotion, and what unique opportunities and contacts you might have to get this book out in the hands of

readers. Some marketing and promotional ideas have long lead times, and it's never too early to start thinking in that direction.

5. It serves as a guide to writing the book (yes, if possible, write the proposal *before* the first draft of the book). Your description of the book in the proposal can keep you on track and prevent you from leaving out parts and pieces you planned to include.

6. Finally, a well-done proposal motivates you through-out the writing process by giving you an image of what the finished product looks like. Your book proposal provides the motivation and encouragement to start writing the book (if you haven't started it yet), to keep moving forward (if you have), to finish the rough draft, and to work through the revisions to a final, polished manuscript.

I want you to know that I practice what I preach. After I published *Writing the Christian Nonfiction Book: Concept to Contract* with Sonfire Media, they asked me to expand my chapter on proposals into the book you are reading right now. What do you think I did, before I put down a single word of the text? That's right—I wrote a proposal.

And in the process, my idea for the book has grown and deepened. My audience is clearer (and larger, for that matter). I have a sharper understanding of the unique facets of my book, and I intend to emphasize those as I write. I am getting some marketing and promotional ideas for the book percolating in the back of my mind as well.

But probably the best part of preparing a proposal beforehand is that I know where I am going with writing this book, and I am jazzed about doing it!

Still Not Convinced? Your Publisher May Persuade You!

There is also the distinct possibility that even if you have a contract, the publisher may want a proposal anyway. Publishers see the book proposal as a *business plan*. It outlines your intended content and your marketing ideas. And it gives some hints to your expectations of what the publisher will provide.

The proposal helps publishers in their marketing efforts, as well. By highlighting the distinctive features of the book and outlining some initial marketing ideas, the proposal gets the ball rolling with the publisher, gets ideas percolating, and from the very start, sets a foundation for a team effort in marketing and promotion between the author and the publisher.

At least, that's how it's supposed to work. You've probably heard many a sad tale of a good book failing in the marketplace because the publisher dropped the ball. Why do these things happen? I'd have to say that it's mostly because the publisher and author never started working as a team. (And dare I add that the first misstep in the relationship may have started with an incomplete or nonexistent book proposal?)

I have known of book projects that were sabotaged by the publisher and author not being on the same page. The publisher had one idea of what the book was about, then at a very late point in the process (such as at cover design) the author made it clear that the thrust of the book was totally different—all because the book was accepted for publication without a complete and well-written book proposal.

At this point I hear the self-publishing gurus chuckle with glee and say, "That's why you should self-publish! Then you can make sure the thrust of the book is what you want it to be." My answer to that is "Well, no, you can't." Unless you, the author, are going to edit and lay out the book, design the cover, and put together a marketing plan *all by yourself*, at some point you have to *explain* the book to someone else, so that they can help you do these tasks. And without a doubt the best way to explain a book is—you guessed it—a book proposal.

A Word to the Novelist

Well, all that sounds fine and dandy for a nonfiction author, but what about a novelist? When I began preparing a proposal for my first novel, I was told by other published authors that a book proposal was a decidedly different animal for fiction. It is three or four times as long (they said), with extensive descriptions of each major character.

Wow, what a lot of work! Beyond that, it seemed impossible for me to write extensively about my characters, out of the context of the story, without it sounding deadly dull. To be honest, the whole procedure discouraged me, so I put my proposal, and my novel, on the back burner for several years.

When I returned to it, I had a few more years of experience, and a little more self-confidence. I decided to try an experiment. I prepared a brief, straightforward proposal for my novel, like the kind I would do for a nonfiction book (and like the kind I teach about in this book), and I started showing it to publishers.

Several publishers showed interest, no one ever asked for anything more extensive, and finally, one publisher sent me a contract. Was it a fluke, or have the requirements for the fiction proposal changed in the last several years?

I posed this question to my friend Nick Harrison, an acquisitions editor for a major Christian fiction publisher, who confirmed that the idea of an extensive fiction proposal is definitely passé. Here's what he said:

Fiction proposal requirements may vary from publisher to publisher. It's always best to check the publisher's website and see if they've posted guidelines for their proposals. If not, the general rule is that the fiction proposal should include a synopsis and the first three chapters of the novel. Some publishers may also want a chapter-by-chapter synopsis.

Notice that Nick mentions various elements in the proposal, such as a synopsis (also known as an overview or premise), sample chapters, and a chapter-by-chapter synopsis. In case you didn't know, that outline sounds a lot like a nonfiction proposal. So if you are writing a novel, don't be afraid to follow the guidelines in this book. (I have been careful to highlight any differences between fiction and nonfiction proposals at every point in the process.) Of course, as Nick says, you should check the submission guidelines of publishers and agents to see if they have any unique requirements for a book proposal. But the outline in this book covers all the items that most publishers and agents ask for.

The Elements of a Complete Book Proposal

That brings us to another question: what are the elements of a book proposal, anyway? Let me stop here and briefly list them. In the remaining chapters, we will discuss them in more detail.

1. Cover Letter

2. Premise Statement (nonfiction) or Plot Outline (fiction)

3. Audience/Market

4. Competitive Titles

5. Author Information

6. Chapter-by-Chapter Synopsis

7. Two or Three Sample Chapters

Since seven is the biblical number for perfection, it would appear that this is a sure-fire recipe for a "perfect" proposal. That may be overstating the case, but if you do a good job with these seven items, you should have all the ammunition needed to pitch your book to a publisher.

The cover letter is, strictly speaking, not part of the proposal itself, but is included with the proposal when you submit it to publishers. The cover letter, along with other parts of the submission process, is covered in Chapter 8. The rest of these elements are discussed in separate chapters (2–7). Finally, Chapter 9 provides sample fiction and nonfiction proposals, so you can see how these principles work out in real life.

Are you ready to take the plunge? Turn the page and jump right in!

What's Your Premise?

It makes sense that the opening pitch of your book proposal should be the premise, because it answers the first question to come to mind: What is your book about?

Can you answer that in one or two short paragraphs—or better yet, one or two sentences? Can you then follow it up with a paragraph or two about the features or benefits to the reader? The premise should not be any longer than a page, single-spaced.

The premise should clearly state what your topic (nonfiction) or plot (fiction) is, what the major elements of your topic or plot are, and why all of this should be of interest to readers. If you write nonfiction, think about what problem your book addresses, and what solution you have identified. If you write fiction, think about the main thrust of the story—the protagonist's goal, obstacles in the way, and the resolution.

The idea is to spark curiosity without revealing the whole enchilada. Don't give away the entire plot, don't reveal every major point, and don't try to prove your argument. It is very easy to end up providing a perfunctory explanation of the solution to the problem in a nonfiction book, so that it appears there is no reason to read the whole book. And of course, in fiction, you only want to tell enough about the plot to make them want to know how it all gets resolved. The goal of the premise is to grab their interest and keep them guessing.

Are You Working under a False Premise?

Whenever I read a proposal for a book, I always want to see the premise first, because it's crucial to the author's presentation. I am also frequently disappointed to discover that the proposal I am reading either has no premise, or it begins with words such as these: "This book will help the reader to …" I'm convinced that the phrase "working under a false premise" must have been coined by an editor!

The premise of a nonfiction proposal should begin by telling your reasoning behind the book, or the need that the book will fulfill, rather than focusing on what the book will do for the reader. That's a fine distinction, but a critical one. If you look at the definition of the word *premise*—something assumed or taken for granted—it may help clarify what you want to say in that section of the proposal. Here is where you want to tell us your presuppositions, the need you saw that inspired you to write the book in the first place.

In a fiction proposal (and in nonfiction proposals for biographies and historical books), it may help you to think in terms of reader *interest* rather than need. Your fiction premise should be a basic synopsis of the plot (which includes primary characters and setting), with a focus on the aspects of your story that will pique the interest of certain readers. And that is where genre comes in. If your story has romance in it, it may appeal to readers of romance; if mystery, to mystery readers; and so on. Aside from these general categories, you may be able to find features in your book that appeal to specific readers. For example, a story where much of the action takes place in a cave may appeal to spelunkers; Latinos may be drawn to a story with Hispanic characters; those with a yen to travel may like a novel set in an exotic location.

A more in-depth look at the audience for the book comes later in the proposal, but your premise should give a hint as to what type of reader will be interested in what you have to say.

Of course you *do* want to include in your proposal what the book will do for the reader (in fiction, perhaps, what the reader may learn from the story), but that comes *at the end* of the premise. Ideally, the beginning of your premise sets the stage for a description of the content of the book, just as the conflict in a novel builds to a climax, when the hero (your book!) comes in to save the day. If you tell what the book will do for the reader without first establishing the need or interest within the reader, your presentation falls flat.

It works the same way in fiction. If your premise tells what a reader might learn from your story before introducing the plot, you make it sound like a tiresome, moralistic tale.

I think some authors skip talking about the need or interest of the reader because they assume that it is obvious—it may be obvious to you, but that's because you've written a book about it. If you're having trouble stating the need or interest for your book in a way that doesn't sound painfully trite, talk to some people who would seem to fit the audience for your book. If you listen carefully, you may gain some insights that will lead you to *revise* your book!

The type of nonfiction book that centers most directly on the need of a particular audience is the how-to book, which says, "Here's your problem or need, and here's how to fix it." It's a great format for a clearly defined audience with a specific need. For example, my book, *Teaching with All Your Heart*, identified Sunday school teachers as the audience and their need to put spontaneity and creativity into a lesson. How did I know that such a need was out there? I talked to other teachers and listened to their concerns—and I looked back at my own struggles and frustrations as a beginning Sunday school teacher.

I am *not* saying that all nonfiction books should be how-to books—what a dull world that would be! What I *am* saying is that you always need to identify a need that your book will fulfill—a need clearly held by an identifiable group of people. The need fulfilled by a non-how-to book, however, may be more subtle and complex, so identifying the need (or interest) of your audience may require that you think it through more carefully. That's why bad how-to books (*How to Solve All Your Spiritual Problems in Three Easy Steps*) are usually bad because they pigeonhole their audience and provide simplistic solutions to complex problems. The author of a book like this probably should have used a different format than how-to!

The fiction form of pigeonholing is to write a story with elements designed to appeal to a specialized audience *without* doing thorough research to integrate the elements into the story and make them realistic, not one-dimensional. No one will be drawn to stereotypes, token characters, or artificial settings. (My pet peeve in this area is where, in historical fiction, a character from a hundred or two hundred years ago talks and acts like a 21st-century person!)

So whether you are doing fiction or nonfiction, be sure to consider your audience and their needs or interests, or you may find yourself, very literally, working under a false premise!

The Twenty-Word Synopsis Challenge

Now that you have your book's premise down to a few paragraphs, let's try something a little more challenging. Quick: can you tell me what your book is about in twenty words or less?

At first blush, that question may seem almost insulting. How can I expect you to boil down your deep, complex masterpiece to only twenty words? But this is not simply a test of how you can handle frustration; there is a reason for getting your idea into twenty words.

One of the most obvious and practical reasons for this exercise is that your publisher will need that statement to sell the book. How many words are in catalog, website, and advertising descriptions of books? Often, it's no more than twenty words or so. And those twenty words often become the foundation for the back cover text. Besides, if you can condense your idea into a punchy sentence or two, you can grab a busy editor's interest in a matter of seconds. You've heard of an elevator pitch? This is a tweet pitch! No editor has an attention span too short to handle that.

It isn't easy to boil down a book that way, but take heart if you are writing nonfiction. A novelist will spend untold hours weaving plot and subplots, character development, suspense, conflict and even a surprise ending into a story, and then the poor soul has to hammer out twenty words that encapsulate his or her story and entice the potential publisher. Nonfiction ideas are often easier to synthesize into twenty words. All you have to do is find the core concept that makes the book unique and meets a need.

My book Concept *to Contract* is a case in point. The full title, *Writing the Christian Nonfiction Book: Concept to Contract* (eight words), goes a long way toward giving you the gist of the book. Hey, I still have twelve words left to tell how the book "teaches an eight-part process to move from idea to published book." (There are my twelve words—I did it!)

Does this tell you everything about the book? Of course not. What are the eight parts to the process? How is writing a *Christian* book different from a secular book? How does this book address the person who has already started writing a book, and is stuck? An editor who has some interest in the book would ask these and other questions, and I have the answers right in my proposal. But that twenty-word sentence gives enough information to get the conversation started.

My first novel, *The Case of the Exploding Speakeasy*, was a bit harder to explain in twenty words, but here's what I came up with: "Sherlock Holmes's smarter brother helps Dr. Watson's son investigate a mysterious explosion and murder in a 1920s Philadelphia speakeasy." That's nineteen words—one to spare—and it covers a lot of ground. It grabs the attention of a specific audience (mystery lovers, and specifically, Sherlock Holmes fans), introduces the two main characters, gives the gist of the plot, and tells us it's a historical novel by identifying the time period and location.

Think about that: twenty words to tell us the main parts of interest to a publisher. Notice how this brief synopsis becomes a microcosm of almost the whole proposal, by telling us the audience, the characters, the plot, and the genre. Those, you see, are the most important elements of my novel. Other parts of the proposal, such as the author biography, are not mentioned, because I only have twenty words to pitch my book, and I'm not important enough to grab any interest. (Sad, but true: I am doomed to obscurity.)

If you, the author, are a famous celebrity, if your name will sell the book, then of course, get your name in the synopsis (and while you're at it, write an endorsement for *this* book, please!). Or, if your position is uniquely relevant to the subject (a book on the 9/11 terror attacks by a first responder, for instance), of course you should include that.

Is a twenty-word synopsis magical? No, not really. But be honest with yourself: if I relaxed that rule, you know that you'd end up with a page-long paragraph of gibberish, don't you? Besides, a twenty-word description is possible. Even if you end up with twenty-three or twenty-four, keep working on it, and I'm sure you can get a single sentence that is twenty or less and sounds better. (I know, because almost every synopsis I've ever written was originally twenty-three or twenty-four words—and the twenty-word version was always better!)

Thinking of the twenty-word synopsis as a microcosm of the best parts of your proposal should help you go a long way toward writing that crucial one-sentence description. But if you're still stuck, it may be because you are focusing too heavily on finding a unique way to describe your book. Start, then, by listing all the things that your book has *in common* with other books. As you start to list them, you will find the book's uniqueness seems to jump out at you.

With my novel, for example, I could talk myself into discovering its uniqueness by saying, "Gee, it's just a book, like everyone else's. No, wait a minute; it's fiction, so that makes it different. And it's a mystery—actually, a historical mystery. It's set in the 1920s, in Philadelphia. Well, the characters are typical aren't they? No, they're based on the Sherlock Holmes stories—Sherlock's brother and Dr. Watson's son. And the plot is a typical mystery, except that it's a murder mystery. Oh, yeah, and it's an explosion that kills the victims. And the explosion occurs in a speakeasy. The victims are the owner of the speakeasy and the guys he's playing cards with."

Slowly I start to carve away at the description of the story, bringing out the words that make it unique: historical, mystery, 1920s, Philadelphia, Sherlock Holmes, Dr. Watson, brother, son, murder, explosion, speakeasy, owner, playing cards. I may or may not use all those words (and in fact I didn't), but at least some of them end up finding their way into the twenty-word synopsis.

Create a Tagline

A premise (fiction or nonfiction) is often preceded by a tagline—a slogan-like phrase or sentence that serves to catch the flavor of the story, while not necessarily giving you a clear picture of it.

James Chartrand (http://www.copyblogger.com/create-a-tagline/) says a tagline for a business or product should capture the essence of your mission, your promise, and your brand. To translate this to a book, it means that a tagline gives your book an identity. When writing a twenty-word synopsis, focus on *description*, but when writing a tagline, consider the *benefits* (nonfiction) or the *unique appeal* (fiction) of the book. Make it short and make it memorable—this time, make it *ten* words or less.

I sure do want to make it hard for you, don't I? But the shorter you can make a tagline, the more memorable. Such grabber phrases are used all the time in advertising to sell everything from Coca-Cola ("The pause that refreshes") to Nike tennis shoes ("Just do it"). And typically, these phrases become trademarks, like those two taglines quoted.

Is a tagline an absolute must? No. But if you come up with a memorable one, it can park your book into the brain of an acquisition editor, and repeatedly bring it to mind. That's great, but what's better is when the book is published, and that slogan parks itself into the brain of the book-buying public.

Ten words or less probably sounds impossible, doesn't it? But (hopefully) you've already come up with a twenty-word descriptive sentence, and you can use that to work with. First, it's a phrase, so it doesn't have to be a complete sentence, which should save some words. Second, it's not *describing* the book, but highlighting the book's *benefits* or *unique appeal* to a specific audience.

Coca-Cola quenches thirst (there's the benefit), and so in four words (count 'em—*four*) the tagline brings to our mind a person stopping to take a drink, cooling a parched tongue and getting a little pick-me-up. All that in four words. Nike goes for unique appeal to their audience by attracting athletes with the advice they've probably heard a million times from their coaches: don't over-think your moves, just go out there and trust your muscle memory to take over when the analyzing part of your brain gets out of the way. Wow! Three words to express an athletic principle, and now every time a coach gives that advice, an ad for Nike runs inside the player's head.

So, I looked over the twenty-word synopsis for *The Case of the Exploding Speakeasy*, and I pondered what was the benefit or unique appeal to a specific audience in this story. I concluded that it was giving Sherlock Holmes fans a chance to see familiar characters in a different historical setting. So I came up with *A Holmes-Watson detective team—in Jazz-Age Philly!* Nine words may not exactly roll off your tongue, but it got some attention.

Concluding Status Statement

Your twenty-word synopsis and/or your short tagline can be placed under the title or subtitle of the book, sort of like a headline for the premise. In a sense, they are optional, but include them if you can. What is not optional—in fact, it is crucial—is a concluding "status of the manuscript" statement. At the end of the premise, in a single sentence, either state that the manuscript is complete, or say how far along you are on the project (30 percent? 75 percent? Rough draft completed and working on revisions?), and when you expect to finish it.

If you have little more than a chapter or two written, just say the manuscript is in process and give a date you expect to complete it. I will warn you that six months is about the upper limit of the patience of most publishers, but if you think you're going to need longer than that to complete the book, don't worry about it. Remember, this is your first draft of the proposal. In Chapter 8, I suggest sending the draft of the proposal around for others to review, and then incorporating their suggested changes. By the time you do all that, the date you've set for completion of the book will be a lot closer!

Who's Your Audience? What's Your Market?

This next step in writing a proposal—a paragraph or two describing the audience and market—is apt to puzzle the average author. The term "market" may draw a complete blank, and if it does, don't worry about it; we'll discuss that in a minute.

But describing the audience may puzzle you as well. If you wrote the premise, you may feel you have already identified the audience. But actually, all you've done is identify the *need* of a particular audience, and not necessarily the characteristics of that audience.

What are most of your potential readers like? What motivates them? Why do they do what they do? What is their age range, educational level, lifestyle, etc.? Where do they hang out? How can you get in contact with them? This section of the proposal should describe what a typical potential reader of your book is like—or, better yet, it could describe several different typical readers.

Go Ahead—Limit Your Audience

I have received proposals with statements such as this in the audience section: "This book about spiritual maturity is for Christians and non-Christians. Its audience is the entire population of the world."

In my rejection letter, I may say something like this: "Have you considered that atheists probably wouldn't be interested in a book on spiritual maturity? Have you considered that unless it is translated, people who read other languages probably won't be interested? Have you considered that many non-Christians, though they may have an interest in spiritual maturity, would probably use a far different definition of 'spiritual' than a Christian would?"

A typical answer I may get to questions like this is, "I'm trying to broaden the market for the book; I'm trying to give you a big target to aim for."

But in reality, such an approach gives the publisher not a big target, but a lot of little ones—more than the publisher can handle—because it is hard to market to a broad spectrum of people, with such a wide variety of needs and interests. Take just one demographic: age. Teens are marketed to differently than retirees, and middle-age adults are marketed to differently than twenty-somethings. But it is possible to transcend age differences if your book meets some kind of need common to people in all those age groups. However, not everyone in each of these age groups will have this same need. Oh, no! You are limiting your audience again! And your publisher will thank you for it.

It is a good thing to limit your audience, because it helps you focus your writing on a more specific target.

The Concept of Felt Needs

Create a description of your audience by identifying the *type* of people who have the need you mentioned in the premise— and who *know* they have that need.

This is the idea of felt needs, a concept you may have heard of before. One of the most common phrases I hear from authors when they pitch their book to me is, "Christians *need* to read this book." Maybe, but do they *know* they need to read it? You can't go into every bookstore and force the customers to buy your book; they have to *want* to. It is your job to prove to the publisher that book-buyers will want to buy your book. The best way (perhaps the only way) to prove that is to identify a need the book fulfills and convince the publisher that people are looking to meet that need.

Fiction Needs

If you are writing a fiction proposal, all this discussion of felt needs probably seems foreign to you, but don't dismiss it too easily. As I said in the previous chapter, a fiction author should look at the word "need" and think "interest." You can argue, of course, that fiction fulfills a need for entertainment, but that is far too general a statement to be of any use. It is better to discuss specific interests of the audience you are aiming at, as well as the genre of the novel.

Once you identify the genre, your typical reader begins to come into focus. Most readers of mysteries, for example, are analytical, and want to match wits with the protagonist in solving the mystery. But you don't have to describe in your proposal what the typical reader of a particular genre is like; the publisher already knows. Your goal in the audience section is to identify the unique aspects of your story that may appeal to readers regardless of genre.

It is possible, of course, that people who fit your protagonist in age, gender, occupation, etc. are going to be interested in your novel. But you probably need to show that your audience would not be *limited* to those who fit your protagonist's description. In addition, you may have some details in your story that would appeal to people of specialized interests. A novel with a lot of its action taking place on a plane might appeal to those interested in aviation; a story set in the Rockies could spark the interest of lovers of that region. It's all a matter of getting a handle on your audience.

You may recall that when I discussed the premise for a fiction proposal, I spoke of features that appeal to specific readers. I gave these examples: a story involving a cave may appeal to spelunkers; Latinos may be drawn to a story with Hispanic characters; those with a yen to travel may like a novel set in an exotic location.

I am *not* suggesting that your novel include "Hispanic spelunkers in an exotic location" as a cheap hook, for the *sole purpose* of appealing to these groups. What I am saying is that you look at your story and determine what unique aspects of it will appeal to a specific audience.

My novel, *The Case of the Exploding Speakeasy*, tells the story of Sherlock Holmes's brother, Mycroft, and the son of Dr. Watson in 1920s Philadelphia. The story grew out of my own interest in the Sherlock Holmes mystery stories, and in my fascination with that era of history. But in writing the proposal for the novel, I realized that Arthur Conan-Doyle's stories of Sherlock have a large fan base—they call themselves "Sherlockians" and they have dozens, if not hundreds of fan clubs around the world. You can bet that I included that information in the audience/market section!

Write to Serve Your Reader

Some authors write a book as pure self-expression, with no thought to meeting the need or interest of a particular audience. They haven't thought about the audience at all.

That approach can lead to a very self-absorbed manuscript. Have you ever listened to a speaker who seems enamored with the sound of his own voice? God save us from that in our writing!

Getting into the skin of your reader—your audience—is an exercise that you should practice every time you write something. Some writing never gets off the ground because it lacks reader orientation. Think about who the average readers of your book will be. Will they understand this information? What practical use will they get out of the material? Why should they care about this? Or to put it more accurately, why *would* the reader care about this? We could write about many things that a reader *should* care about, but *will* they? I call this approach the "Who Cares?" school of writing.

I was once asked to rewrite a wiring installation manual that apparently wasn't communicating well, because it seemed that every time we came to a customer site, the wiring had been installed incorrectly or not at all. The first thing I asked was, "Who's the audience?"

My supervisor looked at me as if I was speaking Pakistani. So I tried again.

"Who is going to read this thing? Who is actually doing the installation, and trying to follow these instructions?"

The maintenance crew, he said. People with experience in installation and repair, but who, like me, would not necessarily understand an overly technical explanation.

I began looking through the manual, which contained pages of wiring diagrams and a long, technical discussion about the phenomenon of "signal echoing." I asked about that and was told the signal "echoed" when the equipment was wired incorrectly.

"In other words," I replied, "it won't work. Why do the wiring installers care about the technical details of why it doesn't work when it's wired incorrectly? Can't we simply explain to them how to wire it correctly?"

After more discussion, I was able to condense the correct wiring method to two simple rules that would be understandable to the average maintenance worker. The revised manual was easier to read and follow, saving our company and customers a lot of time and money—all because I aimed the manual at the right audience.

So it pays to spend some time thinking through what your audience is like, as well as what your market is. You have to step outside your skin to do this. This will help you in the end because it's easier to write to an identified audience than some vague faceless crowd.

Research Your Audience

Research and statistical information can be helpful in fleshing out the characteristics of your audience, but I've seen many an author lose credibility by quoting some generalized statistic and implying that everyone in that statistical group would buy the book: "This book is for married people. Did you know there are X-million married people in the United States?"

On the other hand, you could indicate a potential audience for a Christian book on "how to divorce-proof your marriage" if you show a statistic on the high rate of divorce among Christians. Use of statistics can help you argue the prevalence of the need for your book, but avoid overstating the case. No statistic can guarantee book sales!

And that highlights the difference between the *audience* and the *market* for a book. Audience and market are very similar, but not the same. Audience is what you think of when you are writing the book: who is going to *read* it? Market is what you think of when you are selling the book: who is going to *buy* it?

If you think these two are *always* the same, think again. The audience and market may be identical, but not necessarily. For example, my book on Sunday school teaching will obviously be bought by teachers. Or will it? Although the book is addressed to teachers, it may be purchased in bulk by Sunday school superintendents and Christian education directors— and indeed, it has been. That fact was not important when it came to *writing* the book, but it was immensely important when it came to *marketing* the book — and establishing a market for the book is the purpose of this section.

On some occasions, a book is written for one group of people, but sold to a different group. Books for young children are a great example. Who actually buys them? Adults, not children—parents, grandparents, etc. You want the cover to appeal to a young child, but the content had better be appealing (or at least not offensive) to adults as well, or they won't buy it. Young children might like a picture book that is all about flatulence, but parents probably will be turned off by that. That's why authors seem to reserve the crass and impolite material for children who are a bit older, who have their own spending money, and don't have their reading purchases screened by the adults in their life (even if, perhaps, they should). And now you know why Dav Pilkey's *Captain Underpants* is a success!

Gift books and books designed for volume purchase to churches and other organizations are other examples of a separation between audience and market—those who buy the book give them to others to read. When I write the book, I'm focusing on the person who will read it; when I promote the book, I focus on the person (or organization) who will buy the book. The difference can be subtle, but significant.

Sequels, Subsidiary Rights/Spinoff Products

It can be helpful (but is optional) to include a paragraph discussion of the possibilities of sequels to your book. This issue is likely to be obvious to fiction writers. Maybe your story doesn't really end at the last page. The same characters, locations, and situations may inspire you to a second novel. But if you are writing nonfiction, don't assume that the possibility of one or more sequels is exclusive to novelists. This book, for example, could be the first in a series of Christian writer's guides—covering such topics as brainstorming and outlining, writing the first draft, polishing the draft for final submission, and so on.

Then there's the question of subsidiary rights (selling the right to put your book into another language or medium) and spinoffs (products—usually non-book items—that are based on your book). Here is your chance to dream and brainstorm, but try to temper your imagination. I'm sure every novelist thinks his or her story could be a major motion picture, and every author of a Christian living title feels his or her book ought to be adapted for video or a live conference venue, but try to think about your manuscript objectively.

Are there any specific features to your book that would play well in a different medium? How might your book have spinoffs? Could this lend itself to training courses, videos, a tie-in devotional book, etc.? Don't go overboard with this, but perhaps there are additional possibilities. A quick visit to a Christian bookstore may spark some ideas.

In this paragraph (remember to make it *one* paragraph), it is usually better to lean to the general rather than specific. In other words, you might say that your novel has stage or screen possibilities, and briefly explain why (high-action story, scenic setting, etc.), but don't say that it should be a Hollywood movie with specific actors in the lead roles. (Yes, some authors actually do this!) You may suggest a companion devotional for your nonfiction book, but don't go into specifics on length and content. Remember that you are talking to professionals who are likely to see the possibilities better than you do. The point is to give them something to think about, not to outline an entire plan.

Endorsements

Another optional section is a few short endorsements. If you've finished a first draft of your book, or only the first several chapters, you should show it to a few sympathetic friends—preferably those who are knowledgeable or interested in the subject of your book. If they are prominent (not necessarily big-name, but someone who would command a certain amount of respect), all the better. Compile their responses and determine if there are revisions you need to make in the book, and maybe even in the proposal, based on their reactions. More than likely, however, they will have many positive things to say along with the criticisms. Put those positive statements in your endorsements section.

If you don't have a clearly identified audience and market, you are groping in the dark. If you can briefly and succinctly identify your audience and your market, your proposal and the book manuscript that grows out of it will be well focused and attractive to a potential publisher.

How Does Your Book Compare to Others on the Market?

Book proposals are a thorn in the side of many authors. Much of the information asked for can seem arcane, subjective, and elusive—and to an extent, it is. But arguably, the most misunderstood and mysterious section of the book proposal is the competitive titles section.

The name itself is a problem. It is a misnomer, because one book title does not usually compete with another, at least not directly. So what exactly do we mean by competitive titles?

The mystery begins to unravel when we remember the central purpose of the proposal: to sell the book. The proposal is a request for money—asking the publisher to invest in you and your product, the book. One argument for your book is that it meets a need or fills a gap in the marketplace. (Or, as the snake-oil salesman would say, "There's nothing else like it!") The competitive titles section is designed to do that. It compares your book to others currently in print, showing what makes yours distinctively different.

How is it done? One simple way is to visit the Christian bookstore or an online seller and browse their racks or web pages. Find three or four current books that are somewhat similar to yours. You don't have to buy these books and read them cover-to-cover; usually you can get the author's main thrust by reading the back cover and the table of contents, and maybe skimming the first chapter. In your proposal, include the title, author, publisher, and publication date of each book, with a brief (maybe two sentences) description, explaining why yours is different. Keep your choice current—books published within the last four or five years.

If you find one or more major books that cover exactly the same subject as yours, with exactly the same slant, maybe it's time to rethink your idea. But it's more likely that you will find several books that appear to cover your topic, but not with quite the same angle.

One title can be a bestseller by a well-known author, but don't limit your list to big-selling books. Otherwise you give the impression that your topic is one that is only being tackled by the big names, and the editor will question whether you can compete with Max Lucado or Chuck Swindoll.

You may find a book that is something of a polar opposite to yours—the author comes to a different conclusion, or gives advice you would consider counter-productive, even heretical. Great! You have landed yourself in the midst of controversy—publishers love that! Definitely include that book in your competitive titles section. Just be sure the text of your book addresses the arguments of this author, possibly giving a point-by-point refutation. This is especially important to do if the author of the opposing book is well known.

Now that we have the Internet, there are new possibilities for overwhelming ourselves with too much information. I frequently receive a comparative titles report like this in a proposal: "Amazon.com lists 347 books on this subject, with 147 of those by Christian publishers. I think mine is different because . . ." How can you seriously review 147 titles? This is not seeing the forest for the trees. Limit your review to three or four representative titles. If your book idea is truly unique, it should not be hard to limit the number of titles to three or four that are most similar to yours.

Do a short description of each book, highlighting how yours is different. Then conclude with a short paragraph summarizing what makes your book unique. Choose titles that are deliberately different from yours in some specific way. Then you can use those titles to re-emphasize the distinctive and salient features of your book. That is the ideal competitive titles section: these books serve as a foil, which you play off to show the unique features of your book.

In my proposal for a book on Sunday school teaching (later published as *Teaching with All Your Heart*), I could have wasted my time comparing my book to the literally hundreds of Christian education books out there. But books specifically on teaching Sunday school were less common; books on adding spontaneity and creativity to your lessons were even more rare; and I could find only one other book that specifically addressed using standardized curriculum (and mine was decidedly different than that one). See how a simple comparison to other titles on the market helps you to put the focus on the uniqueness of your book?

I compared my manuscript to three different books. One encouraged teachers to put energy and spontaneity into teaching, but didn't show them how; mine does. One book is biased toward a particular publisher's curriculum (it is written by the publishing company's president, no less!); mine is not. One book does not address the problems involved in using standardized curriculum; mine does.

Did I deliberately choose books that made mine look good in comparison? Of course. But I didn't have to look far to find them; in fact, two were bestsellers in the Christian education market. The moral of that story: if your book is not distinctively different from the biggest sellers on the same topic, you have no business writing it.

In describing how your book is different, there is no need to be combative. You don't have to attack other books in order to defend the legitimacy of your own. In my proposal for *Writing the Christian Nonfiction Book: Concept to Contract,*

I noted that three Christian authors had written books on novel writing, but apparently, no one had done one on writing a Christian nonfiction book. See what I did? Without attacking these other books, I established a market for books on Christian writing and revealed a gap in the market for Christian books on nonfiction.

Finish your competitive titles section with a paragraph that re-emphasizes the distinctives of your book and shows once more that there is a niche in the market for it. As with other parts of the proposal, what you learn from writing this section should help you clarify to the publisher (and yourself) what makes your book unique. Hopefully, that will raise publishers' interest in your project, and perhaps cause you to emphasize those distinctives all the more as you write and/or revise your manuscript. Besides, once you prove that there is a niche in the market for your book, it gives you some strong motivation to get the book done!

CHAPTER 5

Who Are You and Why Are You Writing This Book?

Who do you think you are, anyway?

No, I'm not trying to start a fight and I'm not picking on you. What I am suggesting is that you probably have some thoughts on who you are that don't come out in a typical résumé or biographical paragraph. You should be able to bring those thoughts to the surface by doing a little brainstorming—by asking yourself a few tough questions.

Once you have given yourself the third degree, it probably would be good to pass the job on to a couple of good friends—after all, close friends often know you better than you know yourself. The purpose of all this self-interrogation is to prepare a short (one-half to one page) autobiographical piece for the author information section of your proposal.

It's easy to become stuck on this section of the book proposal, or try to get away with a bland résumé or a canned biographical blurb. Most authors have a hard time seeing what makes them stand out from the crowd. But you need to realize that publishers want to know as much about an author as possible (albeit in as few words as possible!), because they are being asked to invest in this person. They need to be assured that you are worth the investment. For nonfiction writers, they want to know that you have the knowledge and background to pull off a book on this subject. For fiction writers, they want to find social connections and interesting facts about you that may help them market the book.

So dig deep into your life for credentials. What is your ministry in your local fellowship? Do you belong to any organizations? What makes you different from the next person in the pew? The details of your life and experiences that are distinctive may be obscure to you, but obvious to others. One author I worked with did not appear to have the credentials for a book on the spiritual training of children, until she revealed that she had raised three children of her own—and *twenty-five* foster children!

What led you to write this book? Why should you write about this subject rather than someone else? Why did you approach this particular subject in the way you did? What makes you an expert in that area? Don't let the expert label intimidate you; you'd have to have some expertise in that particular area or you'd never have written about it!

Of course, if you are writing a Christian book, you definitely need to have a clear presentation of your personal relationship with Christ. You need to show an expertise in the life of faith. A full-blown personal testimony is not necessary, just some indication that you know this God you speak of. If you have a leadership position or some other ministry in your church, that would be good to mention as well.

Novelists, This Applies to You!

Fiction authors may not realize that they also need to have relevant expertise that makes them the right person to tell their story. I wrote my first novel, *The Case of the Exploding Speakeasy*, about the brother of Sherlock Holmes and the son of Dr. Watson. My expertise consisted of having read every Sherlock Holmes story written by Arthur Conan-Doyle—several times over—as well as many other stories about Holmes and Watson by imitators of Doyle.

My novel was set in Philadelphia, and I lived in suburban Philly for eight years. Where is your novel located geographically? Have you researched this location? (You must have.) Have you traveled to this area? Is your novel historical? What research have you done on that era? I did a great deal of research on the 1920s, the era in which my novel was set. Does your story involve a certain group, subculture, profession? My novel involved organized crime figures, so I read up on them. Does the plot hinge on specific technical knowledge? *The Case of the Exploding Speakeasy* included, not surprisingly, an *explosion*, and since it occurred in an unusual way, I dug into the chemical process involved. I'm not a chemist by any stretch of the imagination, but I was able to learn about it!

Whatever research you've done for your book—fiction or nonfiction—may make you more of an expert than you thought you were.

Consider Your Web of Influence

In what organizations, groups, clubs, etc. do you invest your time? What specific skills and abilities do you have that you have contributed to your community? Do you teach or train others on any subject? Where do you find yourself taking a leadership position? Perhaps in your Sunday school class? Perhaps at community meetings? Perhaps in your profession? If there are people who consider you a leader, these may also be people who would want to read your book.

Dig deep for your contacts and opportunities to market the book. Do you have a website, blog, or other social media presence? Do you speak to any groups during the year? Are you *available* to speak? Can you think of any group of people who would be interested in what you have to say— whether on the topic of the book, or any other topic? Do you know anyone of influence or expertise who might help you promote the book? Brainstorm the answers to these questions with close friends who know you well. You may surprise yourself at how long a list you can create of current or potential groups and individuals who would be interested in you or who could help you promote the book. Don't be surprised if this list begins to overlap some of the information in the marketing portion of the proposal. In this case, a small amount of redundancy is OK.

What I am talking about here is what marketing people call a *platform*. This is your web of influence—people who know you or know about you. You probably have a larger platform than you realize. All you need to do is develop your platform by letting people know you are available to speak on certain subjects, or starting a blog on an interesting topic, or teaching a class somewhere—or all those things and more. For more information on this, I recommend the book *Platform: Get Noticed in a Noisy World,* by Michael Hyatt (Thomas Nelson, 2012).

If you are not a first-time author, you should list your published works—fiction and/or nonfiction; books and/or articles; websites and/or blogs. If you're preparing a fiction proposal, you may not see why it's relevant to include Bible studies you've written or your recent article on parenting. If you're doing a nonfiction proposal, you may think that no one wants to hear about the short stories you've published. But any writing experience shows that you know how to handle the English language, and that's what's important.

How detailed should you be in your writing credits? I've published over 1,000 articles, news reports and fillers over the past thirty years, but I certainly don't list every one of them. Be as detailed about your writing credits as you can be on a quarter of a page. (Of course, you can make it longer if you've published a large number of books.) If you have the sales figures for your published books, it's fine to include them, as long as the numbers are respectable. The figures may be counter-productive if they are low!

It may seem that with all this collecting of information you could write a small volume about yourself, but once you've done this, you need to boil it down to a half-page or a page about yourself and your social network. Some of the information you've obtained may be irrelevant, but you are likely to find some interconnections you never realized existed. When you sit down to tell others about yourself, you may learn some things that even you didn't know.

What's the Outline of the Book?

The last thing you have in your proposal, aside from sample chapters, is a chapter-by-chapter synopsis, also known as the outline section. If you're the type of writer who plans the structure of a book before writing it, this should be a simple process. You simply take the outline you've created and produce a short summary of each chapter. Short means two or three sentences—almost like a premise statement for the chapter.

As I say, a chapter-by-chapter synopsis should be easy if you've already outlined your book. But I'm going to assume that you haven't, because it's a step that many authors tend to skip. A typical response I hear from novice authors, especially fiction authors, is, "I don't outline my book; I just write it and find out how it ends when I finish it."

My response to that is to finish the book or at least a rough draft. Once you do, I guarantee that you will discover information in the first chapter that ought to be in the third chapter, and so on. You will have a confusing and disjointed first draft that could have been written much better if you had outlined it in the first place. And this applies to fiction as well as nonfiction.

Even if you haven't finished the book, you probably have enough of a general outline in your head to be able to write a chapter-by-chapter synopsis. And in writing the synopsis, you may be able to find and correct some of the hitches to the logical progression (nonfiction) or to the plot (fiction) that were hindering you from finishing the book in the first place.

Still, many authors, especially novelists, resist using an outline, for fear of stifling their creativity. In the process of writing, however, there always comes that point of tension. You've developed your ideas and done research to enhance and expand on them. But it's still in a rather disjointed mass. Now you need to organize them into some sort of format, what we usually call an outline. Sometimes, with a shorter piece, you can skip this step and get away with it, because consciously or unconsciously, you are working from an outline in your head.

But for a book, a written outline—which takes the form of a chapter-by-chapter synopsis in the book proposal—is a virtual necessity. Having an outline helps to give a clear structure to the finished book. For a nonfiction author, this is critical for maintaining a logical flow of ideas; for the novelist, a clear structure affects not only the plot, but character development, point of view, and other crucial aspects of the story.

Having said all that, I must admit that outlining can seem to be a major obstacle. If you're anything like me, *outline* is a terror word, dredging up memories of your fifth-grade English teacher, who was determined to teach you how to do an outline properly, even if neither of you survived the process. My English teacher insisted that the structure be precise and symmetrical: every point had to have *three* sub-points, and woe to you if yours had two or four!

No, I am *not* suggesting such a rigid structure as all that— not for nonfiction, and certainly not for a novel. The solution is not to reject outlines altogether, but to produce an outline that works for you—one that will spur you on to complete your writing project. And that is what a chapter-by-chapter synopsis can do for you.

As with the rest of the proposal, the synopsis is a back-and-forth process, a fluid thing, a general mapping of where you are going in this project. As you think more about your book, as you do more research, as you get feedback from others, your proposal should grow and develop; it may be a bit sketchy at first, but it will gradually expand as you learn more and mull over the information you've gathered.

So although you may give this section of the proposal the label of "outline," stop calling it that. Think of it as a writing plan—and ideally, that is what it really becomes. By creating a summary paragraph for each chapter, you break up the project into smaller, more manageable pieces, providing yourself with a clear plan for completing your masterpiece.

The Chapter Synopsis Process

What are the steps in creating a chapter-by-chapter synopsis?

Well, you've already done the first step: in a sentence or two, you've developed a premise statement of what your book is all about—you've put your idea in a nutshell. Now is the time to break the premise down into separate chapters.

Identify the main points (topical points for nonfiction, plot points for fiction) of your premise, which can serve as the *chapters* of the book. Sort through the notes you've made in your brainstorming and research, and these main points should be obvious. After more brainstorming and research, you may add other major points until the list seems complete. Your list of chapters is complete when your research and ideas start producing sub-points rather than entirely new aspects. Nonfiction books are usually eight to fifteen chapters of about 2,000 to 5,000 words each. For a novel, you may have double the number of chapters, but typically somewhat shorter chapters. Nonfiction chapters usually have similar page counts, but chapters in a novel often vary substantially in length. These are general guidelines; they are not set in stone. However, if you have a very long or very short book (under 45,000 or over 80,000 words for nonfiction; under 50,000 or over 100,000 words for fiction), you may have difficulty attracting a traditional publisher or agent.

Next, determine the order of the chapters/sections. If you have a complete list of main points (nonfiction) or a well-developed plot (fiction), a logical progression should be clear. For example, if you were trying to help your reader solve a problem, you wouldn't present the solution without first identifying and defining the problem. After presenting the solution, you probably want to show examples of how your solution works out in real life. If you are doing a biography, you might present the facts in chronological order, by topic, or some combination of the two. A novel should have a plot that builds to a clear climax and a short denouement.

What If I've Already Done All This?

You may already have a list of chapters, or you may have already written a first draft of the book. In that case, look over your chapters and decide if the division and order is as logical as you intend it. For example, you may decide that one of your chapters actually has two major ideas, which might be better expanded into separate chapters. Or you may conclude that two chapters are so inter-related that they can be merged.

In fiction, you may decide that a particular character or scene should be introduced earlier or later to enhance the plot. For example, the editor for my novel, *The Case of the Exploding Speakeasy*, convinced me to bring the explosion into the story earlier, which helped hook the reader in those critical first pages.

As with every part of the proposal, the chapter-by-chapter synopsis can be considered tentative until the final revision stage. I can say for myself that the chapter division and order of almost every one of my books has been altered a little between the first draft and the final version.

But don't let the tentative nature of your chapters stop you from creating a synopsis. Once you have the chapter divisions and order in a stable form, create a single-paragraph description of each chapter, keeping the premise section at your elbow as you write.

Be clear and complete in these paragraph descriptions, but also be brief—and keep them guessing. Include enough information to fully describe the chapter, but don't go into needless detail. You want readers of the proposal to wonder how you handled that dramatic scene or explained that difficult concept—so they want to read the book! One thing that works well in a nonfiction chapter description is to mention a number, such as "five vows for spiritual power," without enumerating what they are. This sparks curiosity, so that a publisher is more likely to read the manuscript.

In fiction, there is a major exception to this principle: agents and publishers want to know how your story *ends*. As one editor I know puts it, "I want to know all the spoilers. That is the only way I can determine if the storyline is going to work." While I agree with that, I want to emphasize that conciseness is the key. In the synopsis of my novel, *The Case of the Exploding Speakeasy*, I clearly showed when and how the killer is revealed in the appropriate chapter, but not specifically *who* the killer is. To reveal the killer's identity would only lead to complex details surrounding motive and method, and the resulting chapter descriptions would have been too long. Work hard to make your descriptions short, subtle, and effective. I often use descriptive phrases rather than complete sentences in a chapter-by-chapter synopsis, in order to make it as concise as possible. Here, for example, is a chapter paragraph from the proposal for *Concept to Contract*:

> How to prepare an outline you can use as a *writing plan*, instead of the way you were taught in school. How outlining fits in with research. How to avoid the "same old, same old" tendency in outlining.

After you finish the chapter-by-chapter synopsis, review it and make sure it hangs together as a unit, with a clear introduction, body, and conclusion. This is probably a good time to pull out your premise and compare it to the synopsis. Make sure you produce chapter descriptions that fulfill the promises of the premise.

A well-written chapter-by-chapter synopsis will serve as a guide for writing the chapters. Whenever I write a book— fiction or nonfiction—I always put the paragraph description at the top of each chapter, so it's right there in front of me when I write. (This is, of course, a temporary placement; once I've finished the chapter, I remove the description.)

Many times, this practice has helped me to remember to add details to a chapter that I might otherwise have forgotten.

A Note to Devotional Writers

At the risk of contradicting everything I've said about the chapter-by-chapter synopsis, I must advise you to forget the traditional synopsis format if you are writing a daily devotional, especially a one-year plan. No, you don't need to prepare 365 descriptive paragraphs. (I have actually received proposals like that, and I was sorry the authors went through so much unnecessary work!)

For a devotional synopsis, describe in detail the format of daily entries. For example, you may begin each entry with a passage of Scripture; the body of the devotional entry may include a memorable anecdote; and you may conclude with a prayer or a thought for the day.

Also explain any unique features to the devotional, such as thematic patterns. The content of the entries may follow the seasons, with winter stories featured in February and summer stories in July; or, each month may cover a different theme.

Don't forget to mention any other items in the devotional, such as an index.

Overall, the synopsis for a daily devotional book is quite flexible, as long as it shows the book's unique features and overarching theme.

CHAPTER 7

What Samples Can You Include?

The final section of the book proposal is two or three sample chapters (or selections) to give the agent or publisher an idea of the flavor or tone of the book.

I know—this sounds inconsistent, doesn't it? All through this book, I've advised you to prepare the proposal before you write the first draft. So how can you have a couple of completed chapters to include in the proposal?

The answer is simple: you can start working on your first draft before you are done with the proposal, so that you are working on both simultaneously. That way, by the time you finish with the proposal, you already have a couple of chapters done, as well, and you can submit the chapters with the proposal as a single package.

If you haven't begun work on the book yet, it's no big deal. Just start writing your first draft, and in the meantime show the rest of the proposal to several people to get their feedback.

By the time you've written a couple of chapters, you may have revised the proposal based on the feedback, and you'll have a stronger presentation to show to potential publishers.

This is a major reason to prepare your proposal before writing the book—you want to answer questions and address objections now instead of later. (It's easier to rewrite the proposal to incorporate some issue you failed to address than to rewrite the finished manuscript!)

Show it to a couple of people who fit the description of your audience (and if you can't find two people who fit, you need to rewrite the "Audience" section!).

Show it to a couple of people who might be considered experts in the field you are writing about. I don't necessarily mean PhDs, I just mean someone with expertise. Show a proposal for a book on evangelism to someone you know who is a real soul winner, for instance—someone who probably could have written the book.

Show it to other writers and editors—a Christian writer's conference is an ideal place to do that.

Ask for and expect honest criticism and suggestions for additional material. Then weigh the suggestions carefully, considering the source. For example, if a college professor tells you it's too popular or not academic enough, remember that this poor soul spends hours poring over research papers and dissertations. If a person with little or no experience in writing tries to give you tips on grammar, smile and nod politely. But if an editor makes suggestions about your writing craft, your intended audience, or your marketing strategies, you probably want to listen!

Editorial Checklist for Authors

Once you have two or three chapters written, you should take them through a revision process so that these samples are less like drafts and closer to being publication-ready. (And remember to edit your proposal as well.) Complete the checklist below and you will be putting your best foot forward.

✓ Quoted material: Provide credit information (author, title, city, publisher, date, page number) for all quoted material.

✓ Lengthy quoted material: You may need to obtain permission for use of *longer* material and for poetry and song quotes of *any* length. (FYI, most publishing contracts stipulate that the author must pay any fees charged for use of quoted material.)

✓ Bible translation: Identify what Bible translation you are using for quoted passages of Scripture. If you are using more than one, identify the alternate translations. It is probably best to limit your usage to no more than three translations, with one translation used the majority of the time.

✓ Formatting issues: The page margins should be one inch. Use a 12-point, serif font, such as Times New Roman for the main body text. Use a header or footer on each page with the book title and your name, address, phone number and e-mail (you can make this as small as 9-point type). Also, include the page number in the header. The body of the proposal should be single-spaced, but double-space the sample chapters.

✓ Typesetting issues: Are your dashes, quotes, etc. correct?

For example:

	Incorrect	Correct
Em-Dash	home -- after	home—after
Apostrophe	Bob's	Bob's
Quotes	"house"	"house"

Make sure your opening quotes have closing quotes—otherwise, the editor has to *guess* where the quote ends!

✓ Bible verse typesetting: Please be sure all quoted Bible verses are exactly as printed in the Bible version. For example, if the word "Lord" or "God" is in small caps (LORD, GOD) you need to type it in that way as well. If a long passage has paragraph breaks or is set in separate lines like poetry, type it in that way. Some of these rules have been relaxed in recent years and may vary by the version you are quoting or whether your book is scholarly or informal. Always refer to The Christian Writer's Manual of Style for details on quoting Scripture correctly. The publisher's website may also state their preferences for Scripture quotations.

✓ Graphics: Do you have any illustrations or photos with the sample chapters? If so, remove them from the word-processing file, and put them in separate, high-resolution graphics files.

✓ Special elements: Are your captions, quotes at the start of chapters, discussion questions, and other repeated elements clearly marked and consistently placed throughout manuscript?

✓ Footnotes or endnotes: Endnotes are usually preferred over footnotes by most publishers. Endnotes should be in a separate file, numbered consecutively by chapter. Use superscripted numbers in the text of the book to indicate an endnote, like the "1" at the end of this sentence.[1] Do not use your word processor's automated endnote program. Automated endnotes don't always translate over from one program to another, so the information in the endnote can be lost.

✓ Text in text boxes: Remove any text (such as sidebars) from boxes and put them in the body of the manuscript, for the same reason you want to remove automated

endnotes. You can include a note for the graphic designer

before and after the text like this:

<<begin sidebar text>>

Text of sidebar.

<<end sidebar text>>

How Do You Pitch This?

There is one thing left to prepare before your proposal is complete and ready to send around to publishers: you will need a cover letter.

The cover letter is a one-page business letter with a few abbreviated highlights from the rest of the proposal, so it should be the last thing you write. Find the three most persuasive points in your proposal and mention them in the letter. Better yet, hint at them. If you can spark some curiosity with your cover letter, it's done its job.

But before I tell you about cover letters, let me tell you about another type of epistle that is virtually the same in content, but with a distinctively different purpose: the *query letter*.

Getting Past the Catch-22 of Publishing

Remember the movie *Catch-22*? (Well, neither do I; I was just a kid when it came out, and my mom wouldn't let me go to an R-rated movie!) The title comes from a fictitious rule in the military bureaucracy that said that a fighter pilot could be released from a dangerous mission by pleading insanity. The catch to the rule was that pilots asking to get out of a dangerous mission must not be insane—so they were no longer eligible!

An apparent catch-22 of publishing hampers most beginning writers: you can't get published unless an editor looks at your book proposal, but more and more publishers do not accept unsolicited manuscripts or proposals!

The solution to this conundrum is the query letter. This is a description of the book in a way that will spark the editor's curiosity, but is brief enough not to waste the editor's time if it's not right for the publishing house.

For a good query letter, all you need are three or four paragraphs:

Paragraph 1: Hook them with a problem, a story, a question. Make sure it's a good one. If it's a problem, it needs to be important, with universal appeal. If it's a story, it has to be a grabber. If it's a question, it has to be compelling. *Don't* use a question that begins with, "Did you know . . . ?" The editor is likely to respond, "No, I didn't know that, and I don't care." Or worse yet, "Yes, I do know that, and I don't care." And into the wastebasket it goes!

Some authors use the first paragraph of the book's introduction or first chapter for this kind of opening hook. That can work very well sometimes—and if it doesn't work, you should ask yourself why not. If that paragraph doesn't grab the editor in the query letter, maybe it's not the best way to begin the introduction or first chapter, either!

Paragraph 2: Present an abbreviated version of your *premise* and two or three of your most telling sub-points from the proposal. Don't, however, give away the whole gist of the book—not only do you not have space to do this (keep it *short*), but you want to spark their curiosity. (Remember the twenty-word synopsis challenge? Here is a good place to dust that off and try it out.) In other words, you might say you have stories illustrating how to keep your faith fresh, but don't tell the stories. Numbers are always good; for example, you may say you have five simple steps for improving one's prayer life, but don't say what the steps are. The editor should be curious enough to read the sample chapters to find out what they are.

Paragraph 3 (optional): You might tell the editor—briefly—a little about yourself. Don't give your entire history from kindergarten to the present. Just explain what makes you qualified to write this book.

Last paragraph: Give details about length (your word count) and approach (first-person vs. third-person, casual vs. formal style, etc.). Do you envision the format as an e-book, a printed book, or both? If printed, do you see it as a soft cover, hardcover, or gift book? (Since most printed books are standard-sized soft cover, you had better have a good reason to get creative with the format.) Also add that you are willing to make changes in length, style, and format as required. Then tell the publisher that the manuscript is complete, or if not, give a date when it will be ready. (Don't tell a publisher that you need more than six months to get it done, or your query will probably be rejected.) Finally, you conclude by asking if the publisher would like to see the proposal, and end with, "I look forward to hearing from you."

Most importantly, remember the three rules for query letters: brevity, brevity and brevity!

When you get a response from a publisher to send the proposal, include a *cover letter*. A cover letter is almost the same as the query letter, except that at the beginning you should thank the publisher for being willing to look at the proposal and sample chapters, and at the end you of course do not ask if they want to see the proposal (obviously, they do!).

One of the great things about a query letter is that you can send it off to several publishers at once, and improve your chances of a positive response. And if you receive a request to send your proposal, your chances of being published are increased substantially. You've broken through the catch-22 of publishing!

Marketing Your Manuscript

Marketing a manuscript—peddling your creation to publishers—is the point in the process that I dread. I try to find shortcuts for it—and I've regretted it many times. So if you're smart, you'll learn from my mistakes and start the following marketing plan as soon as you have a workable version of your proposal:

1. **Send your query letter to multiple publishers.** Check a market guide (such as *The Christian Writers Market Guide*) and writers' guidelines for several publishers. Feel free to send a query simultaneously to any publishers who are looking for books like yours and who specifically say they accept queries. (Don't worry—this is NOT the same as a simultaneous submission. Publishers do not expect a query letter to be sent to them exclusively.) It is not unusual to send a query to a dozen publishers, but make sure you customize the letter for each one—no "Dear Publisher" generic letters.

   The vast majority of publishers are willing to receive e-mail queries, and in that case, use the text of your query letter as the body of the e-mail. If your publisher wants a letter by postal mail, include a self-addressed, stamped postcard for the publisher to say yes, they want to see the proposal, or no, they don't.

2. **Send a proposal to all who respond positively.** At this point, you need to check if they will accept simultaneous submissions of proposals. Publishers who refuse to consider a simultaneous submission may mean complete manuscripts only; others mean proposals as well. If you can, send it to multiple publishers. As I said before, the cover letter should differ from the query letter in that you begin by acknowledging that they asked for the proposal: "Thank you for giving me the opportunity to show you my proposal . . ." Send the full manuscript if the publisher asks for it and you have it completed. If you have to send a proposal or manuscript to a single publisher, make sure you emphasize that fact in your cover letter: "This submission is being sent to you *exclusively* . . ."

As with queries, many publishers accept proposals and full manuscripts by e-mail, but if you are required to send a hard copy, include your e-mail address for a response and tell the publishers that the manuscript can be disposed of when they have finished reviewing it.

3. **Take several copies of the proposal to writers' conferences.** Most Christian writers' conferences have opportunities for ten- or fifteen-minute free appointments with an editor, as well as more in-depth critiques for a reasonable fee. Try to meet with editors who are looking for manuscripts like yours, but any editor can provide a general critique of your work. Take advantage of these opportunities to receive feedback from publishing professionals.

4. **Based on the feedback you receive, revamp the proposal as needed.** If an evaluation—or even a rejection—includes some positive comments, add them to the revised proposal. Probably the simplest way to do this is to put a subhead such as "reader comments" and quote the editors verbatim, with their names and job titles. No need to go into how it was rejected, simply note the positives.

5. **Keep good records.** Mark down where and when you sent the query, proposal, or manuscript, and when you received a response.

6. **Finally, don't be discouraged.** It may take several rounds, several revisions, and several months (perhaps *years*) to find a home for your manuscript. Nobody said it would be easy!

If you follow this process diligently, you have a good shot at being published. If you don't follow these steps, you are likely to waste a lot of time. I speak from experience!

In marketing your manuscript, you may sometimes hear advice about customizing your proposal to the particular publisher you send it to. This may be a useful thing to do, if you are sure that you know what unique things that publisher is looking for. For example, I have submitted a proposal to a denominational publisher, and highlighted my connections to that denomination.

There are limits to this practice however; you don't want to change the thrust of the premise, for example, thinking that it will appeal to this publisher. It is far better to submit your proposal to an appropriate publisher. Find a publisher that fits your book; don't alter your book to fit a publisher. I've tried that, and trust me, it never works!

What Does a Proposal Look Like?

Often it helps to see an actual proposal that you can use as an outline. Included in this chapter are the proposals that sold my nonfiction book, *High-Wire Teaching—Without a Net: How to Customize Your Sunday School Curriculum for Creativity, Spontaneity and Effectiveness* (re-titled *Teaching with All Your Heart*), and my novel, *The Case of the Exploding Speakeasy*. I've inserted a few notes within these samples to point out or further explain features.

And, as a special bonus for purchasing this book, visit my webpage (http://fromconcepttocontract.com/) to download free fiction and nonfiction proposal templates to guide you in preparing your own proposal. You'll find a sample of a proposal cover letter that can be downloaded as well.

[NOTE: Cover page. Title centered. Larger font. Times New Roman font. Subtitle centered. Smaller font. Contact information follows author's name.]

High-Wire Teaching—
Without a Net:

How to Customize Your Sunday School Curriculum for Creativity, Spontaneity and Effectiveness

[NOTE: Although you have a title for your book when you write your proposal, it is a working title. Your publisher will likely change the title to enhance marketing. My title was changed to Teaching with All Your Heart when published. Yes, it's true—so don't become too attached to your title if you are seeking a traditional publishing contract.]

by

David E. Fessenden
123 Main Street
Anytown, USA 54321
555-555-5555
dave@fakeaddress.com

PROPOSAL

High-Wire Teaching—Without a Net:

How to Customize Your Sunday School Curriculum

for Creativity, Spontaneity and Effectiveness

by

David E. Fessenden

[NOTE: Remember to single space the body of the proposal. Sample chapters will be double-spaced, however.]

PREMISE

[NOTE: This paragraph sets up the problem; the paragraphs that follow explain the solution provided by the book. Other possible formats besides problem and solution (which works best with how-to books) include beginning and end for a chronological biography, and conflict and resolution for an issues book.]

Many Sunday school teachers are frustrated with their curriculum—but not as much with the content as with the format. How can they cover all the steps in the lesson? If class time runs short, what do they cut out? How can they infuse creative ideas into a standardized lesson?

High-Wire Teaching—Without a Net: How to Customize Your Sunday School Curriculum for Creativity, Spontaneity and Effectiveness encourages the teacher to take control of the structure and direction of the lesson, and not be intimidated by the curriculum.

In an upbeat, nonacademic style, this book counsels teachers to use the standardized lesson plan as a guideline rather than a strict checklist. Through a series of simple organizational and memorization techniques, *High-Wire Teaching— Without a Net* explains how to present a lesson without repeatedly referring to notes or the manual. This approach allows a teacher to bring a spontaneity and excitement to the lesson that is otherwise difficult to achieve.

With practice, this method of preparation and presentation can be applied to greater teaching challenges, such as elective classes based on a popular Christian book. The final chapter shows how to prepare meaty, engaging lessons even with *no* teacher's manual or study guide.

[NOTE: More than simply identifying the audience, this section shows that the audience has the same need you have described in the premise and that they know they have that need.]

AUDIENCE

This book specifically addresses the Sunday school teacher's challenge of working with standardized curriculum; this is its most potent selling point. In the midst of today's busy schedules, many Sunday school teachers become frustrated trying to adapt their teaching style to even the best standardized curriculum. Much of their limited preparation time is spent trying to follow the curriculum writer's train of thought, and they have little energy left to be creative. Most Sunday school teachers and superintendents would be attracted to a fresh, practical, and efficient approach to preparing and presenting a lesson. The methods taught here are adaptable to teaching any age group.

It is likely that this book will *not* appeal to those teachers who would never consider departing from the text of the teacher's guide, who are fearful of innovation. I believe these teachers are in the minority, and may even be won over as they realize that customizing curriculum is practical, easy, and just plain fun.

[NOTE: These are only a few of the books I could have included. I chose these for their ability to highlight the distinctives of my book.]

COMPETITIVE TITLES

After contacting Christian bookstores and asking Christian educators to recommend books on the subject of teaching, several titles have come to my attention. The following are examples:

1. *Bore No More!*, by Mike and Amy Nappa (Group, 1995). This title is very popular among Christian educators. Surprisingly, it contains nothing more than a collection of

"sermon ideas" with some suggestions as to how to present the material. I believe its appeal is centered in its lack of structure and detail. Because the specifics of the "lessons" are not spelled out, the teacher is forced to customize them to his or her class situation and teaching style. Not all teachers are able to do this with success, however. The whole premise of High-Wire Teaching—Without a Net is to train the teacher to succeed at customization of curriculum.

2. *Why Nobody Learns Much of Anything at Church: And How to Fix It*, by Thom and Joani Schultz (Group, 1994). This book is on the right track in that it discusses the issues involved in teaching with standardized curriculum, but the authors have a distinct bias: Thom Schultz is the president of Group Publishing, a curriculum publisher. Most standardized curriculum, they say, is dull and out of touch. Their solution? Group Publishing's curriculum! *High-Wire Teaching— Without a Net* does not attack standardized curriculum; nor does it endorse any particular publisher. The methods are intended for use with any curriculum.

3. *You Can Teach Sunday School with Success*, by Daniel Schantz (Standard, 1994). This book contains a broadbrush approach. Single chapters on preparation and presentation do not address the problems involved in teaching with standardized curriculum.

Conclusion

While existing books discuss preparation and methods, there is little emphasis on the *presentation* aspect of teaching.

The common problem of implementing creative ideas into standardized curriculum and adapting a lesson to different types of students and teaching styles is not comprehensively addressed. Other competitive titles that could be named are older, backlist material by authors with advanced degrees in Christian education. While they contain much that is good, their approach is often pedantic and unappealing to the average Sunday school teacher.

Sunday school teaching should be an exciting, energetic, and engaging ministry. My goal in *High-Wire Teaching— Without a Net* is to free teachers to use their creativity for conveying the timeless truths of Scripture. I believe in standardized curriculum and I do not endorse one publisher over another.

ABOUT THE AUTHOR

David E. Fessenden is the managing editor for Christian Publications, Inc. in Camp Hill, PA. He is also editor of *The Alliance World*, a quarterly missions' education journal for The Christian and Missionary Alliance. His teaching and speaking experience includes industrial training programs, professional workshops, and local church Sunday school classes from toddlers to adults.

[NOTE: Endorsements can be acquired by sending a draft version of the proposal to beta readers (those readers who read the proposal or manuscript before the final edits). If you can, choose people who have expertise in the topic of your book.]

ENDORSEMENTS

The Christian educators I contacted were excited about the concept of *High-Wire Teaching—Without a Net*, and recognized its unique approach. The following are a few of their comments:

You have done a wonderful job of bringing together many helpful ideas which can only serve to improve and enhance the teaching skills of anyone who reads the book. Your style is fluid and well structured, your thinking lucid, and your suggestions practical and sound.

Dr. Kenneth O. Gangel, Executive Director, Toccoa Falls College, Graduate Studies Division

As a Christian educator who conducts about twenty Sunday school evaluations a year, the problem of how to use curriculum correctly has become a glaring icon of frustration. . . . This is a book I would purchase by the case and distribute to my churches. It is right on target in meeting the needs of the local church teacher.

Rev. Joseph Burchill, District Director of Christian Education, Christian & Missionary Alliance

I have never met a Sunday school teacher who was totally satisfied with any given curriculum, and "if teacher ain't happy, ain't nobody happy." Your book helps them view the teacher's manual as a guide rather than a rulebook and frees them to develop their own God-given style of teaching. . . . I love the style of your writing. It's so readable and catchy and just pulls you along.

Shirley G. Brosius, Adjunct Lecturer in Christian Education, Evangelical School of Theology

Anything we can do to encourage teachers to personalize and customize their lessons is welcome. Teachers need to understand that curriculum—any curriculum—is simply a resource, a guide, a tool for them to use. And as with any tool, they use the tool; the tool doesn't use them! . . . I sincerely believe you are working on a valuable resource for teachers.

Marvin Parker, National Director of Christian Education, Christian & Missionary Alliance

MARKETING ISSUES

While I believe *High-Wire Teaching—Without a Net* has good potential in the retail bookstore market, I can think of at least two other possible markets:

1. *Volume sales to denominational Christian education departments*, which typically put a high priority on the

training of Sunday school teachers, but often lack practical, readable training materials. Many are more than willing to look outside the denomination for such materials.

2. ***Teacher training seminars***, using *High-Wire Teaching— Without a Net* as a textbook. A one-day seminar could be conducted at almost any local church that is large enough to have a viable Sunday school. My background in industrial training gives me the expertise to launch such a ministry regionally and to train others to do it nationally. A number of churches in my area have already approached me about conducting a one-day seminar.

OUTLINE/CHAPTER SUMMARY

Introduction

A short vignette of three types of teachers leads into a discussion of the difficulties encountered when teaching with standardized curriculum and briefly describes the organizational method for solving the problem.

Chapter 1: Where Do You Fit In?

This chapter exposes the preconceived notions we often have about Sunday school teachers, and reassures those who may not feel they measure up. You can be an effective teacher, even if you don't "fit the mold." The secret is in learning to customize your curriculum.

Chapter 2: A Map of the Territory

That every lesson should have a beginning, a middle, and an end should be an obvious concept. Yet, as this chapter shows, this truth appears to be ignored by some curriculum writers. The structure of the three-part lesson format is presented with an explanation of how the simplicity of the outline builds creativity and spontaneity into the lesson.

Chapter 3: Customizing the Lesson

This chapter demonstrates how to overlay the three-stage outline onto standardized curriculum, adapting the content of the lesson to this natural presentation format. What style of teacher are you? What style of learners are the students in your class? This chapter helps you identify yourself and your students so that the lesson can be adapted appropriately.

Chapter 4: Rightly Dividing the Word

Using the tips in this chapter, you can learn how to quickly analyze the scriptural foundation of a lesson, how to add Bible content to strengthen a weak lesson and other ways to "teach the Word." Also included are suggestions on using Bible study resource materials in lesson preparation.

Chapter 5: Hooks to Hang Truth On

An overview of various teaching methods is given in this chapter, with explanations on how to use a different method—or even a combination of methods—for each stage of the lesson. Further explanation of the nature of the three lesson stages is shown in the process.

Chapter 6: The Words of Your Mouth

Following the example of Jesus Christ (undeniably the world's greatest teacher), the ancient but still effective practice of *asking questions* is described here, along with other techniques of oral presentation. This chapter draws heavily on the Gospels to find the secrets behind creating provocative discussion questions, using effective transitional statements, and answering students' questions.

Chapter 7: It's Show Time!

This chapter covers the actual presentation of the lesson, including organizational and memorization techniques for keeping the main points of the lesson in your head. Teaching without repeatedly referring to notes or a teacher's manual is a bit scary, but the chapter explains how to make that tension work to your advantage.

Chapter 8: Monday-Morning Hindsight

Techniques are presented for conducting a healthy self-evaluation of the lesson, based on notes you take *as you teach*. This chapter also shows how to get useful student feedback, even from the youngest of learners, and how to apply what you've learned to the next week's class.

Chapter 9: Creating Your Own Curriculum

This chapter brings together the major points of the book and shows how to apply these techniques to other teaching challenges, such as an elective class based on a popular book or a Bible study—even if no teacher's guide is available.

Appendix: Teaching Methods List (Optional)

Bibliography (Optional)

Leader's Guide (Optional)

Estimated completion date for the manuscript is September 2000. The completed book will be approximately 30,000 to 35,000 words.

PROPOSAL

The Case of the Exploding Speakeasy

by

David E. Fessenden

[NOTE: Typically, a novel does not have a subtitle, so here is a space where you can do a short description of the book, giving genre, market, theme, and other specific information.]

A Sherlock Holmes-inspired mystery novel for the CBA market in which a murder mystery is woven together with an exploration into the mystery of faith

[NOTE: Twenty-word synopsis of the story, followed by a tagline.]

Sherlock Holmes's smarter brother and Dr. Watson's son investigate the murders at a card game in a 1920s Philadelphia speakeasy.
A Holmes and Watson Detective Team
—in Jazz-Age Philly!

[NOTE: "Premise" could be labeled "Plot Outline" if you prefer. Optionally, this could be preceded by a list of main characters and a sentence or two description of each.]

Premise

Thomas Watson left London two years ago and crossed the Atlantic to become a newspaper reporter in Philadelphia— 1920s Philadelphia, a city that rivals Al Capone's Chicago for its corruption. Why would he go so far from family and friends? Admittedly, he was trying to get away—away from the shadow of his famous father, Dr. John Watson, and his father's even more famous friend, Sherlock Holmes. Shortly after Thomas leaves London, Sherlock dies, and Dr. Watson takes on the responsibility of caring for Sherlock's older brother, Mycroft.

After two short years in which Thomas finds little success in journalism, Dr. Watson dies suddenly; though Thomas stands to inherit his father's estate, he is also saddled with the responsibility of Mycroft, who has mysteriously shown up in Philadelphia, ready to move in.

Puzzled by this strange turn of events, Thomas takes a walk—and suddenly finds himself caught up in the biggest story of his career—a suspicious explosion at a speakeasy, which kills the owner and his card-playing buddies.

Thomas is needled into making a bet with a rival reporter on the motive for the apparent murder. In addition, the principal suspect of the police is Basil Meridan, a former British butler whom Thomas befriends and Mycroft hires as a servant. All this makes it necessary for him to solve the mystery, or lose his money and his friend.

It doesn't prove to be easy. Thomas's investigation is hampered by his editor, who fires him for spending too much time on a "dead-end" story (a misunderstanding that appears to have been orchestrated by his rival on the paper). As he attempts to recover from this setback, he is escorted against his will to a meeting with bootlegger "Boo Boo" Hoff (an actual historical figure) and his goons. They also want to know who the killer is, and provide their own unique "encouragement" for Thomas to find the solution to the mystery.

Thomas and Basil search the offices of Harry Ragan, the owner of the speakeasy, but they are interrupted by the police and narrowly escape arrest. As a result, they are unable to retrieve anything more than Ragan's personal ledger and appointment book. These items appear to contain little relevant information, but Mycroft considers them very significant—though he won't explain why. One thing the ledger shows is Ragan's contributions to—of all things—the local city mission! (Modeled after the well-known Philadelphia institution, Whosoever Gospel Mission.)

Thomas goes there (and Mycroft uncharacteristically decides to come along) to talk to the director, "Captain Bill," a Salvation Army worker. Surprisingly, Mycroft knows him from his work with Sherlock, when the captain was known as "Willie the Touch," a safecracker. (A recurring irony in this and later volumes in the series is that Mycroft, a supposed newcomer to Philadelphia, knows far more people in the city than Thomas, who has lived there for two years and is virtually friendless.) At this point, Thomas discovers, much to his chagrin, that Mycroft "got religion" years ago—in fact, he was the one that led Captain Bill to the Lord!

With a new roommate and a butler, Thomas's small apartment seems even smaller, but his inheritance enables him to consider the purchase of a house. Captain Bill and his daughter, Margaret (Maggie), live in an apartment on the second floor of a large house, which just happens to be for sale. By the end of the day, Thomas finds that he has become a homeowner—and a landlord!

This close association with unabashed "holy rollers," and the shocking discovery that Mycroft is among them, is too much for Thomas (who, despite his attempts to be seen as a hard-boiled newspaperman, is still very much a proper Englishman). He decides that he will have to look into this issue of religion. But first, he has a mystery to solve.

From the scanty clues Thomas provides, Mycroft solves the mystery, but is tight-lipped about the solution—after all, Thomas should be able to figure it out himself! Eventually, by accident, Thomas stumbles onto the murderer—and nearly becomes his next victim.

[NOTE: A series is often more attractive to a publisher than a single novel, so if you have firm ideas for sequels (or prequels, for that matter), include them here with a one-paragraph description of each. Note that I leave the number of books in the series open-ended with a general paragraph about additional books in the series. If your work is a stand-alone novel, don't force it into a series mold; this section is optional.]

Series Synopsis

This is the first of a series of Mycroft Holmes/Thomas Watson novels.

- In Cry Wolfe, Thomas agrees to meet with Nicholas Wolfe, a member of the Philadelphia Crime Commission and a Mainliner—a member of Philadelphia high society. When he shows up for the appointment and finds Wolfe dead, Thomas promptly reports the murder to the authorities. Then Wolfe shows up alive, and accuses Thomas of seeking free publicity for the paper. Thomas must solve this mystery or be discredited and disgraced. In the process, Thomas learns who his real friends are and comes to a crisis of faith.

- The third book in the series will see Thomas reporting on the citywide revival meetings being conducted by a flamboyant evangelist (modeled after Billy Sunday and Paul Rader). Thomas's newfound faith seems to clash with his instincts as a reporter, especially after the evangelist is accused of fraud. In the same novel, Thomas's friendship with Maggie will develop into something more serious, despite his best efforts to avoid it.

- A fourth book will center on the theft of jewelry owned by Sarah Drexel Van Rensselaer, the richest woman in Philadelphia. (This was an actual crime that occurred in the 1920s.) After a personal struggle, Thomas proposes to Maggie.

- Additional books in the series will chronicle further mysteries, set within Thomas's struggles as a newlywed, as a young Christian and (note the change of career) as an English professor at Philadelphia Bible College. Each volume in the series will address issues of faith—set in the context of the rich history of the 1920s, but relevant to today.

[NOTE: While author information in a fiction proposal is mainly focused on the author's web of influence, note that I have also established my expertise in the Sherlock Holmes stories.]

About the Author

David E. Fessenden is an independent editorial and publishing consultant, having served in editorial management for CBA publishing houses over the past 20 years. Dave has a B.A. in journalism, an M.A. in theology, and 30 years experience in writing and editing. In previous positions, Dave served on the communications staff of Elim Bible Institute and was editor of a regional edition of the largest Protestant weekly newspaper in the country.

Dave has published five books: one fiction, and four nonfiction. He has also produced study guides for two titles by A.W. Tozer, published modernized versions of classic bestsellers, written hundreds of newspaper and magazine articles, and edited numerous books.

For ten years, he was a regular columnist for the Christian writers' newsletter, *Cross & Quill*, and is a frequent workshop leader at Christian writers' conferences. His teaching and speaking experience includes industrial training programs, college-level continuing education seminars, and professional writing workshops.

Dave and his wife, Jacque, have two adult sons and live in Harrisburg, Pennsylvania. Dave is an avid fan of mysteries, with a special interest in Sherlock Holmes. He has read every one of the Conan Doyle novels and short stories, and numerous pastiches by various authors.

[NOTE: The marketing section identifies both a general market (mystery) and a specialized market (Sherlock Holmes fans) for the book. The fact that mysteries are popular is obvious to a publisher or agent who deals with mysteries (and I would not submit this to anyone who does not handle mysteries). So I make a general statement about the popularity of mysteries in general, and Sherlock Holmes in particular, but I don't belabor the point.]

Marketing Issues

Special Features/Benefits: The Sherlock Holmes mysteries by Arthur Conan Doyle, and the resulting pastiches and parodies by various authors, continue to fascinate new generations of readers. The CBA fiction market is very favorable toward mysteries, and a series that continues the story of Conan Doyle's characters would be welcome. In addition, the religious milieu of the 1920s has some parallels with the state of the church today. The Mycroft Holmes/Thomas Watson series affords opportunities to comment on trends and issues in the church from a fictional perspective.

Author Promotion: I speak at a number of Christian writers' conferences every year, and I preach several times a year at various churches, promoting my ministry with CLC International. There is no reason why I cannot include my novel on the display table and mention it in my speaking. In addition, I can provide a promotional website and send notice of the novel by e-mail to several hundred friends and acquaintances. I am eager to do what I can to promote the book.

Endorsements: Early versions of chapters of the novel were read in Patricia Rushford's fiction class at the Oregon Christian Writers summer conference several years ago, with a positive response. I am hopeful that the contacts I gained there will give me an opening to obtain endorsements from Patricia Rushford, Bette Nordberg, Mark Littleton, and other novelists in the CBA market.

[NOTE: While publishers and agents know that mysteries are popular, they may not know about Sherlockian fan clubs. But I do, because I've done some market research.]

Markets: While this novel series would be mainly a CBA title, it is possible that the popularity of Sherlock Holmes would allow for crossover into ABA. There are a large number of Sherlockian organizations throughout the country, and I have contacts with several in the northeast. It is possible that the novel series could be promoted through these outlets.

Subsidiary Rights: It is also possible that the series could generate interest in the TV/film/stage rights, just as there have been many stage and screen adaptations of the original Sherlock Holmes stories and their resulting pastiches and parodies.

[NOTE: Competitive titles are handled differently for fiction; rather than list other mystery novels I have simply written a paragraph that explains what makes my story unique. I specifically compared my novel to only one other title (footnote), and only to show why mine is different.]

Competitive Titles

To the best of my knowledge, no CBA author has tapped into the rich literary vein of Arthur Conan Doyle's Sherlock Holmes canon, with one recent and questionable exception[1]. Since I have read all the Conan Doyle novels and short stories, as well as several pastiches and parodies, I have the background to do this. Also, in dealing with Sherlock Holmes "once removed"—Sherlock's brother and Dr. Watson's son—I can retain some of the flavor that will attract Sherlockian fans, while adding in a faith element that might be difficult to insert into a true pastiche that is faithful to the original stories. (Doyle tended to be a secularist at the time he wrote the stories, and later a spiritualist.)

The series I propose would remain true to Arthur Conan Doyle's creation, while maintaining the historical accuracy of the 1920s, and providing a plausible and logically solved mystery.

1   The only recent author to have taken the Doyle characters into the CBA market is L. Frank James with his book An Opened Grave (Salt Works, 2006), in which Sherlock Holmes and Dr. Watson go back in time to investigate the resurrection of Jesus Christ. The premise of the book is entirely foreign to the Sherlock Holmes saga, especially the science-fiction angle of time travel. In addition, because the book was released by a Christian publisher, the final outcome is no surprise and could hardly be considered a true mystery. The novel has received mixed reviews on Amazon.com.

[NOTE: Most publishers and agents will consider an uncompleted nonfiction book, but do not want to look at a fiction proposal unless the finished manuscript is in hand.]

Status of Manuscript

The manuscript is about two-thirds completed, with all major plot problems and technical issues ironed out. I expect to complete it by the end of 2012.

The Case of the Exploding Speakeasy

Chapter-by-Chapter Outline

PROLOGUE

Former English butler Basil Meridan, now a waiter in a speakeasy, attempts to bring drinks to his boss's back-room card game. Finding the door locked, he stumbles to the kitchen, shortly before the back room explodes.

CHAPTER 1

Introduction of narrator, Thomas Watson, only son of Dr. John Watson, the companion of the late and celebrated detective, Sherlock Holmes. As a newspaper reporter in 1920s Philadelphia, he has the unpleasant task of writing his own father's obituary. On returning to his apartment, he finds that the door is unlocked, and he hears someone moving about inside; with a trembling hand, he opens the door and steps across the threshold.

CHAPTER 2

Thomas discovers that Mycroft Holmes, Sherlock's "smarter" brother, has arrived from England, expecting to be provided a place to live. After some discussion about this turn of events, Thomas goes for a walk to clear his head.

CHAPTER 3

Thomas runs headlong into the explosion at the speakeasy, and attempts to cover it for the paper. In the process, he meets Basil and brings him home for a cup of tea.

CHAPTER 4

On returning to the apartment, Mycroft surprises Thomas by greeting Basil as an old friend of his, then surprises Basil by asking for details on the explosion at the speakeasy— before Basil or Thomas have a chance to tell him. The next day, Thomas turns in his story, which is rejected, because the waiter's testimony sounds implausible to the editor. The story is handed over to Larry Jones, who immediately proclaims it a mob hit. Jones then offers to convince the editor to let Thomas back onto the story, if Thomas will make a bet with Jones on the outcome. Against his better judgment, Thomas agrees.

CHAPTER 5

On returning home, Thomas is confronted by Mycroft, who deduces that his editor didn't believe his story, and offers to help solve the mystery. Thomas takes a trip to the coroner, and studies the bodies. He discusses the case further with Mycroft, who proposes that the explosion was due to "a combustible atmosphere, but not a gas." What is that supposed to mean? Thomas begins to wonder if Mycroft is beginning to show signs of senility.

CHAPTER 6

Meanwhile, Thomas decides that more information is needed—but how can he get back to the scene when the cops have shut down the speakeasy? Basil comes to his rescue with a set of keys to the building. Soon they are in Harry Ragan's office—but before they can do any searching they are confronted by Officer Feeney, who wants to know why they are there. Backed up against the office desk, Thomas in desperation reaches back and stuffs something up the back of his coat. After he and Basil leave the building, he checks it. It turns out to be an appointment book. Basil was also able to secret something out of the office, but he has not done much better—it's a personal expense ledger.

CHAPTER 7

The ledger and appointment book reveal little—meetings with suppliers, appointments with the dentist, payments for booze, showgirls, etc., etc. Thomas notices how Ragan seems to have his personal finances and his business mixed together. Mycroft points out that the significance of the appointment book and ledger is not as much what is in them, but what is missing. Thomas realizes he is trying to drop a hint, but he doesn't want to play the "student-professor" game.

CHAPTER 8

Molly, a flapper who used to hang around Ragan's place and is always flirting with Thomas, says she knows a secret about Ragan—he used to show up at the services at the city mission. When Thomas wants to follow up on the lead, his editor fires him. He decides to go to the mission anyway, and Mycroft, in an uncharacteristic burst of energy, goes along. They meet Captain Bill—whom Mycroft knew in London as Willie "the Touch," a safecracker. Here is where Mycroft's faith is revealed—and to Thomas's mind, this confirms his suspicion of senility.

CHAPTER 9

Captain Bill invites them back to his apartment to meet his daughter, Margaret (Maggie). It comes out that the house is for sale, and before he knows it, Thomas is the new owner of a large house with an upstairs apartment!

CHAPTER 10

Maggie takes Thomas to the owners of the building to discuss the deal. Afterwards, Maggie invites him to a service at the mission, and he reluctantly agrees to go. Molly happens to see Thomas on the street with Maggie and embarrasses him. Maggie, however, takes an interest in her and invites her to the mission.

CHAPTER 11

Thomas sits through a special service at the mission (with the Billy Sunday-type evangelist preaching), mostly just to please Maggie. He also thinks he may be able to write it up for the paper. Captain Bill tells him more about Ragan's card-playing buddies, who were always laughing at him for his interest in the mission. Thomas notes that one of the regulars—a guy named "Painless"—was not there that night. When Captain Bill starts to talk about spiritual issues, Thomas "suddenly remembers" that he has to leave. Molly is nowhere to be found, but Captain Bill promises to make sure she gets home safely.

CHAPTER 12

Thomas returns to the paper for his final paycheck, and is offered his job back if he produces a decent concluding story on the explosion. Shaking his head over this twist of fate, he leaves for lunch—and suddenly is hustled into a car and taken to a warehouse, where he meets the bootlegger "Boo Boo" Hoff. Hoff tells him to keep looking for the killer, and to let him know when he figures it all out—,"then I'll take it from there."

CHAPTER 13

Following this unsettling experience, Thomas has to endure the gloating of Larry Jones, who is convinced that he has already won the bet. He returns to the apartment very discouraged, and is even more unsettled by the fact that Mycroft and Basil are in the midst of moving his belongings to the new house. But Mycroft gives him a ray of hope by pointing out that if "Boo Boo" Hoff doesn't know who the killer is, then it almost certainly is not a mob hit, or he would be in the thick of it. All that remains is for Thomas to prove that theory—if he can.

CHAPTER 14

Basil mentions that he knows where Ragan's bookkeeper, a Mr. Bemish, lives, and Thomas goes to see him. The man pulls a gun on him, which Thomas manages to wrestle away, and then gets some good information out of him.

CHAPTER 15

Meeting with Basil, Thomas reviews all their information, and determines that there must be someone else they can get information from. Basil mentions that Ragan's dentist uses laughing gas, and Thomas decides to go see him. Perhaps Ragan said something while under the influence of the gas.

CHAPTER 16

Watson goes to see the dentist, and in the process is almost murdered by the killer, but is saved by Basil (who is sent by Mycroft when he realizes that Thomas has misinterpreted the clues!).

CHAPTER 17

Wrap-up of mystery by Mycroft, with Thomas on the couch, still a bit weak from his experience. As it is all explained, he suddenly realizes that he has to get to the office and write this up, before Jones does! Jumps up and leaves. As he heads out the door, he hears Mycroft saying, "Where does he get all his energy?"

CHAPTER 18

Thomas writes the story, hands it in, and confronts Jones, who tries to weasel out of the bet, but this time, the editor stands up for Thomas, and makes Jones pay up.

CHAPTER 19

Final scene with Thomas, Basil, Maggie, and Molly sharing a meal at an Italian restaurant. Basil toasts Mycroft, to Thomas's chagrin.

Suggested Reading

Fessenden, David E. *Writing the Christian Nonfiction Book: Concept to Contract.* Galax, VA: Sonfire Media, 2011.

Goss, Leonard. *The Little Style Guide to Great Christian Writing and Publishing.* Nashville: Broadman & Holman, 2004.

Hudson, Robert. *The Christian Writer's Manual of Style.* Grand Rapids: Zondervan, 2010.

Hyatt, Michael. *Platform: Get Noticed in a Noisy World.* Nashville: Thomas Nelson, 2012.

Ide, Kathy. *Proofreading Secrets of Bestselling Authors.* Raleigh, NC: Lighthouse Publishing of the Carolinas, 2014.

About the Author

David E. Fessenden is an agent with WordWise Media and an independent editorial and publishing consultant, having served in editorial management for CBA publishing houses over the past 20 years. Dave has a B.A. in journalism, an M.A. in theology, and thirty years experience in writing and editing. In previous positions, Dave served on the communications staff of Elim Bible Institute and was editor of a regional edition of the largest Protestant weekly newspaper in the country.

Dave has published six other books, four nonfiction and two fiction:

The Case of the Exploding Speakeasy (Lighthouse Publishing of the Carolinas, 2013)

Writing the Christian Nonfiction Book: Concept to Contract (Sonfire Media, 2011)

Teaching with All Your Heart (Cook Communications, 2002)

A Light to All Japan—children's version (Christian Publications, 1998)

The Waiting Missionary (Christian Publications, 1995)

Father to Nobody's Children, the Life of Thomas Barnardo (CLC Publications, 1995)

He has also produced study guides for two titles by A.W. Tozer (published in the back of the books), written hundreds of newspaper and magazine articles, and edited numerous books. For ten years, he was a regular columnist for the Christian writers' newsletter, *Cross & Quill*, and he is a frequent workshop leader at Christian writers' conferences. His teaching and speaking experience includes industrial training programs, college-level continuing education seminars, and professional writing workshops.

Dave and his wife, Jacque, have two adult sons and live in Harrisburg, Pennsylvania.

Visit Dave's website for information about his editing services and to download your free sample cover letter and book proposal templates. While there, subscribe to his blog to receive ongoing hints for writing for the Christian market. ***fromconcepttocontract.com***

CPSIA information can be obtained at www.ICGtesting.com
Printed in the USA
BVOW08s0447090615

403750BV00003B/8/P

CPSIA information can be obtained at www.ICGtesting.com
Printed in the USA
BVOW08s0447090615

403750BV00003B/8/P